Walt Disney's Cartoon Magic

Walt Disney lived on a farm when he was a young boy. From an early age, walt liked to draw animals. He watched the farm animals carefully he made lifelike drawings of them. Walts family had no money for paper but Walt was clever. he drawed a pig on the wall of his house. Walt's parents were not happy! Then Walts aunt gave him drawing paper

WATCH FOR

• apostrophes

MONDAY	WEEK 1

When walt grew up, he got a job drawing animuls for animated cartoons. creative ideas filled Walts head. the other cartoons were silent so Walt made a cartoon with music and talking characters. This cartoon was called <u>Steamboat Willie</u>. The star was mickey Mouse. Mickey talked and singed, people loved him

WATCH FOR

• apostrophes

TUESDAY	WEEK 1

Walt liked to try new things. most cartoons were only a few minutes long. Walt wanted to make a two-hour animated film. some peopil said it was a bad idea but Walt believed in himself He made Snow White and the Seven Dwarfs. The Audience cheered at the end. as they leaved the theater, they hummed "Whistle While You Work.

• titles of movies and songs

WEDNESDAY   **WEEK 1**

Disney's new ideas changed animated films forever He was full of energy and over the years maked many popular cartoon films. People have been watching Peter Pan, Bambi, and other disney films for years. people will watch them fer years to come. they'll keep singing songs like When You Wish Upon a Star.

• titles of movies and songs

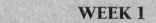

THURSDAY   **WEEK 1**

FRIDAY　　　　　　　　　　　　　　　　　　　　　**WEEK 1**

Write about a person you know. Tell about something special that the person did. Tell about the person's childhood, teenage years, or adult life. Use words that tell what the person is like. Tell how the person's actions made a difference to other people.

_____

_____

_____

_____

_____

_____

_____

_____

_____

The Search for Planets

Planets are large objects in space they travel around the sun. In earlier times, people thought there were six planets They knew about Earth, mars, and venus. They knew about mercury, jupiter, and saturn. Was anything else out there Early telescopes were too weak to spot other planets

- names of planets
- questions

MONDAY   **WEEK 2**

march 13 1781, was an important day. F. william herschel and caroline L herschel discovered a seventh planet they called it uranus They wondered if there were still more planets out in space Some people thought so. They kept looking because they were curious

- names of people and planets

TUESDAY   **WEEK 2**

jean J. Le Verrier thought he knew where another planet was he asked johanne G galle and heinrich L d'Arrest to look for it. That very night, they thought they saw something. What was it By the next night, they new that it was a planett. Thanks to their work, neptune became the eighth known planet on september 24 1846

WEDNESDAY   **WEEK 2**

What was beyond neptune Dr. clyde W tombaugh found out. He discovered pluto on february 18 1930. It became the ninth known planet in 2006 scientists decided it was to small to be a planet. If all gose well, a spacecraft will fly past pluto in 2016. It will take pictures the pictures should tell us a lot. Are there more planets in our solar system What do you think

THURSDAY   **WEEK 2**

FRIDAY   WEEK 2

Tell what you know about how the last two planets were found. Give their names and tell who found them. Write the dates when they were found. Use one of these topic sentences, or write your own:

- Uranus and Neptune are the last two planets to have been discovered.

- Curious scientists discovered the seventh and eighth planets.

_____

_____

_____

_____

_____

_____

_____

_____

Letters to an Author

604 W tabb lakes Dr

yorktown VA 23693

february 24. 2004

Dear Mrs faith ringgold

My name is sara, and I am in the third grade Our teacher, ms. brock read Tar Beach to us. i likied it a lot

MONDAY   **WEEK 3**

Ms: brock said that your drawings are story quilts that you painted. I like the way they look in tar beach i read Cassie's Word Quilt to my little sister, erma. I can't wait to read the rest of your books

Sincerely

sara T sanchez

TUESDAY   **WEEK 3**

813 E cactus St

portland TX 78374

may 7: 2004

Dear Mrs faith ringgold;

     i found your song, "Anyone Can Fly, on your Web site My teacher Mr cohen, let me teech it to the class

WATCH FOR

• address
• commas
• song titles

WEDNESDAY   **WEEK 3**

     Everyone in the class liked "anyone can fly." i hope You write more songs mr. cohen is now reading The Invisible Princess to us. The story quilt drawings are wunderful. Next, i am going to read bonjour, lonnie

     Your fan

     lakeesha R wilson

WATCH FOR

• commas
• book and song titles

THURSDAY   **WEEK 3**

Write a letter to Mrs. Faith Ringgold. Tell her what you like about her books and drawings. Tell the names of some of her books. Be sure to include your address, a closing, and your name. Use one of these closings, or one of your own:

- Very truly yours,

- Sincerely,

- Your fan,

_____

_____

_____

_____

_____

_____

_____

_____

A Salty History

Did you know that salt is a mineral that forms in the ground The salt that is removed from salt mines is a rock called "halite." You are really sprinkling tiny rocks on your food. When you use a salt shaker You can also get salt from seawater The oceans salt is very pure Many people think it tastes bettar than table salt. Mmm. which salt do you prefer

- questions
- apostrophes

MONDAY   **WEEK 4**

Do we need salt Yes, we do. Our cells need salt to stay alife. As a matter of fact, salt makes up nearly one percent of our bodys blood and cells. Salt is used to preserve foods because it kills germs salt is also used to make glass soap, and other items. one kind of salt is used in popular ice-cream machines.

- questions
- apostrophes

TUESDAY   **WEEK 4**

          Daily Paragraph Editing • EMC 6803 • © Evan-Moor Corp.

Polands famous salt mines are very inusual. For hundreds of years, miners have dug salt from deep beneath the Earths' surface. They have carved elegant rooms and beautiful statues from the solid salt curious tourists visit to see the miners statues. wow would you like to see them

- questions
- apostrophes

WEDNESDAY   **WEEK 4**

Across the ages and arownd the world, salt has been valued very highly it was important and hard to obtain. The ancient Roman soldiers' wages were paid in salt Their word for "salt" was "sal" That is where our word "salary" come's from. Gee, would you like to get paid in salt In many places, salt is still a symbol of friendship

- questions
- apostrophes

THURSDAY   **WEEK 4**

Write what you know about salt. Tell where it comes from and how it is used. Explain why people need salt. Tell some interesting or unusual things abut salt. Use one of these topic sentences, or write your own:

- Salt is an important mineral.

- For ages, people all over the world have used salt.

- Did you know that salt has been used instead of money?

_____

_____

_____

_____

_____

_____

_____

_____

Barcodes

What is a barcode Look on the bottom of a cereal box. Do you see a group of black bars and spaces That's a barcode A barcode identifies a product. The thin bars thick bars and white spases are used in a different way for each product

• questions
• commas

MONDAY   **WEEK 5**

Where are barcodes used The first barcodes were used in supermarkets. Clothing toy book and other stores also use them now. the barcodes help stores keep track of what they sell. Eech item in a library has a barcode. The post office uses barcodes to track mail

• questions
• commas

TUESDAY   **WEEK 5**

How is a barcode read A barcode reader reads the code A laser beam in the reader reeds the pattern of thin lines thick lines and spaces. It translates the pattern into numbers. The numbers are sent to a computer. The computer stores the information

WATCH FOR
- questions
- commas

WEDNESDAY   **WEEK 5**

Can barcodes be used with people or animals Yes. Barcodes are used in hospitals blood banks and offices. Hospital barcodes have facts about the patients. Blood banks use barcodes to label the bludd. Some companies use barcode ID cards for their workers. Researchers put barcodes on animals

WATCH FOR
- questions
- commas

THURSDAY   **WEEK 5**

Write what you know about barcodes. Be sure to tell what they look like, how they are read, and where they are used. Begin with one of these topic sentences, or write your own:

- Barcodes are a helpful invention.

- Barcodes are used in many ways.

- What do you know about barcodes?

_____

_____

_____

_____

_____

_____

_____

_____

The Grand Canyon

The Grand Canyon is a long deep cut in the land. it is about 448 kilometers (278 mi) long It goes across northern arizona. stand allong the wide flat rim Look down into a vast rugged wilderness see rocks that are millions of years old. the layers of rock look like colorful striped pancakes

• commas
• abbreviations

MONDAY   **WEEK 6**

some parts of the grand canyon have steep rocky slopes There are no trees or plants. Othar parts have short stubby bushes. columns of rock up to a mile (5,280 ft) high reach up from the canyon floor The Vulcan's Throne is a volcano cone. it rises 172 meters (567 f.t) from a rock shelf

• commas
• abbreviations

TUESDAY   **WEEK 6**

The northern rim is the coolest wettest part of the Grand canyon. it has harsh freezing winters The coldest month is january There may be up to 130 inches (11 f,t,) of snow on the ground the hotest month is july. less than 15 centimeters (6 in) of rain fall during the hot dry summer

- commas
- abbreviations

WEDNESDAY   **WEEK 6**

The colorado river flows along the bottom of the Grand canyon. it looks like a slick winding ribbon! most of the river is about 15 meters (50 ft,) deep After a rain, the river is a muddy reddish-brown kolor. the river has about 40 kilometers (25 m.i.) of swift foaming rapids The rest of the river flows at a calm slow pace

- commas
- abbreviations

THURSDAY   **WEEK 6**

Describe the Grand Canyon or another place you know well. Tell where it is. Include words that tell what the place looks like. Put two adjectives next to each other in one sentence. Be sure to put a comma between them. Begin with a topic sentence like one of these, or write one of your own:

- The desert is a hot, dry place.

- There's a lot to see in the park.

- My neighborhood is an interesting place.

_____

_____

_____

_____

_____

_____

_____

News on the Wing

WATCH FOR

- names of people and places
- commas
- dialog

Butterflies Return to mexico

february 21 2003

Theres a forest near mexico city mexico. Why are the trees black and oranje? Its the wings of 500 million monarch butterflys. Scientists tourists and locals are thrilled. mrs elva m cruz said Oh theyre so pretty! They come in october and leave in march."

MONDAY   WEEK 7

WATCH FOR

- names of people and places
- commas
- dialog

january 2002 was a tough month in mexico. There was hard rane frost and very cold weather. Sadly, three-fourths of the butterflies died. dr juan r campa said, Some of them lived. We didnt know what would happen to them. Luckily, they flew to texas florida and other states. Their offspring have now come back."

TUESDAY   WEEK 7

Robins Flock to virginia

february 23 2003

Usually, virginia has some robins. This february, there are millions more. dr greg k Hill said Many of these birds are from states like georgia. They go to new jersey new york and other northern states for the sumer. Theyll stop in virginia, and then fly on.

- names of people and places
- commas
- dialog

WEDNESDAY   **WEEK 7**

dr hill also said that december january and february were very cold. The ground in the Northeast is still frozen. The birds cant find worms insects or any other food there. Theyre staying in virginia instedd of flying north. Folks in richmond yorktown and norfolk are happy. mrs b k marks said Wow I love their singing.

- names of people and places
- commas
- dialog

THURSDAY   **WEEK 7**

Write a summary of the news article about butterflies or the one about robins. Tell where and when the story takes place. Tell what happened and why. Begin with one of these topic sentences, or write your own:

- Something important happened in (Mexico, Virginia).

- There's good news from the (insect, bird) world today.

- Nature is putting on a good show in (Mexico, Virginia).

_____

_____

_____

_____

_____

_____

_____

_____

_____

Rosie's Diary

WATCH FOR
- colons in time
- dialog
- exclamations

wednesday june 9. 2004

dear diary

On tuesday night, dad came home from work at 7:15 p.m. He walked in sat down and kicked off his shoes. He said, I need a vacation. Let's go to aunt Mimis house at the beeche. I want to leave at 1-00 p.m. on friday"

mom said great Ill call Aunt mimi now.

MONDAY	WEEK 8

friday june 11- 2004

dear diary

WATCH FOR
- colons in time
- dialog
- exclamations

what a terrible day I got up at 658 a.m. We ate breakfast packed the car and waited. The pet sitters bike had a flat. We didn't leave until 942 a.m.

every ten minnits, pete said are we there yet, dad? We finally arrived at 5;26 p.m.

TUESDAY	WEEK 8

saturday june 12 2004

dear diary;

    this morning at 9"14 a.m. I rode my cousin Mikes bike to the beach. It was beautiful. I swam collected shells and read. soon, the rest of the family joined me.

    I asked, auntie, can we watch the sunset tonight?

    aunt mimi said "sure We'll come back at 730.

WATCH FOR
- colons in time
- dialog

WEDNESDAY   **WEEK 8**

monday june 14 2004

dear, diary

    we went out in my aunts boat. at 11,13 a.m., I saw four dolphins. Wow We took pictures sang and chatted. I told aunt mimi that i didn't want to leev.

    She said "you can stay here until july 1st. mom and dad nodded I yelled "hooray!

WATCH FOR
- colons in time
- dialog

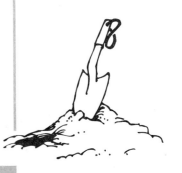

THURSDAY   **WEEK 8**

FRIDAY   **WEEK 8**

Choose one of these ideas and write a diary entry:

- Write an entry for June 10th. Tell what you did to get ready for the trip.

- Write an entry for July 1st. Tell what you did on the last day of your vacation at the beach.

- Write a diary entry about your own life. Tell about something that you did or how you felt about something.

_____

_____

_____

_____

_____

_____

_____

Recommended Reading

- titles of books
- commas

have you ever dreamed about being a hero Well the kids in Defenders of the universe a book by D V Kelleher make that dream come true Each kid has a secret identity a costume and a talent. For example, Packrat carries a lot of things in her backpac. the names are clever and the costumes are great

Defenders of the Universe

MONDAY   **WEEK 9**

- titles of books
- commas

The friends are just playing at first but then they see a womann get hit by a car. The driver doesnt stop The kids use their talents and they help the police find the driver. How? Read the book to find out It has suspense humor and mystery. The kids sound like real kids. honestly, you'll like Defenders of the Universe.

TUESDAY   **WEEK 9**

do you like riddles? Do homonyms like "cents," "sense" and "scents" confuse you? If so, the book called Eight ate: A feast of homonym riddles by M terban is for you. The riddles are clever and the pictures are funnie. Also, the answers explain the meanings of the homonyms Youll think, laugh and learn when you read this book

WATCH FOR
• titles of books
• commas

WEDNESDAY   **WEEK 9**

are you too old for an alphabet book No youre not "the icky bug alphabet book" by J pallotta has interesting facts humor and realistic pictures. Some of the bugs in this book include a ladybug a horsefly and a tarantula. Youll learn a lot and have fun, too. Really, you wont want to Miss this icky book

WATCH FOR
• titles of books
• commas

Defenders
of the
Universe

THURSDAY   **WEEK 9**

FRIDAY   **WEEK 9**

Write a review of a book you like. Give the title of the book. Tell who wrote it. Give the names of the characters, and tell something about the story. Explain why you like the book, and say why you think others will like it.

_____

_____

_____

_____

_____

_____

_____

_____

Historic United States Capitals

Dover delaware, is the capital of the first state in the United states. The second-oldest state house is there. Dover was named for dover england. Mr eldridge johnson was born in dover. Did you know that he invented one of the first record players! In may, Dover celebrates its history with a big fair called Old dover Days.

- names of places and people
- questions

MONDAY **WEEK 10**

President abe lincoln was born in kentucky. When he was a young boy, he moved with his family to indiana. He later settled in springfield illinois. Mr lincoln, Mrs Lincoln, and three of their children are buried there. Many tourists come to see Lincoln's home and grave. In february, theres' a Lincoln birthday weekend. There is a big parade. Doesnt that sound like fun

- names of places and people
- questions

TUESDAY **WEEK 10**

Would you like to see juneau alaska Youll have to go by boat, airplane, or dog sled! Juneau doesn't have any roads. Its' the only U.S. capital like that. The City was started in 1888. It was named for M.r. joseph juneau. He and others found over $158 million worth of gold there. Do you like folk festivals juneau has a great one in april

WATCH FOR

• names of people and places
• questions

WEDNESDAY   **WEEK 10**

honolulu hawai`i, is the capital of the newest state. It has the oldest wooden house on the islands. The only palace in the U.S. is there. Two rooms in the capitol building look like volcano cones. Theres a museum for the battleship USS Arizona. It sank in nearby pearl harbor. Wouldn't you like to surf in the pacific Ocean off hawai`i

WATCH FOR

• names of places and ships

THURSDAY   **WEEK 10**

Write about one of the historic United States capital cities. Remember to capitalize the name of the city and state. Give some interesting facts about the city. Use a contraction in your paragraph. Begin with one of these topic sentences, or write your own. Fill in the name of the city.

- ____ is an interesting city.
- ____ is historic for many reasons.
- The city of ____ is full of history.

Kids on the Go

Wanda Know rights for the magazine kids today. here, she interview Bea Gone of the organization Travel Kids

WK: Where did you celebrate presidents' day

BG: That was february 17 2003. We toured George Washington's home at mount vernon virginia. We sang yankee doodle dandy and ate cherry pie.

- questions
- titles of magazines and songs
- holidays

MONDAY   **WEEK 11**

WK: Where did you go for independence day

BG: We went to philadelphia pennsylvania, on july 4 2003. We watched a parade and sang the star spangled banner. We saw a movie called 1776. We took a tour of the USS Olympia. It's a historic ship and museum. During the fireworks, we sang "its a grand old flag

- questions
- titles of movies and songs
- holidays
- names of ships

TUESDAY   **WEEK 11**

WK: Where did you go for Earth Day on april 22 2004

BG: We went to san francisco california. We read "the Earth book" to school kids. We sang every living thing.

WK: Wasn't that written for Earth day's founder

BG: Yes. We heard more abowt John McConnell while we toured the bay aboard the Golden Gate Cruiser.

WATCH FOR

- questions
- titles of books and songs
- holidays
- names of ships

WEDNESDAY   **WEEK 11**

WK: Did you go to lincoln nebraska, for arbor day

BG: Yes. arbor day began in nebraska. We went there on april 25 2004. We planted treas in a new park.

WK: Did you read poems like trees and "Evergreen.

BG: Yes, and we saw a movie called all about arbor day.

WK: Thanks for the interview. I'll talk to you again soon?

WATCH FOR

- questions
- titles of poems and movies
- holidays

THURSDAY   **WEEK 11**

Write some more questions and answers for Wanda Know's interview with Bea Gone of the Travel Kids. Ms. Know might ask Bea about how the Travel Kids spent St. Patrick's Day, Columbus Day, Veterans Day, or Thanksgiving. Bea could tell about where the group went and what they did. Be sure to use capital letters for the names of holidays, months, places, and people.

_____

_____

_____

_____

_____

_____

_____

_____

_____

John Glenn, Space Hero

John glenn was the first American to orbit Earth in a spacecraft. The Friendship 7 was launched from Cape Canaveral, florida, on february 20 1962. It went around earth three tims. Then it splashed down in the atlantic Ocean. The United States Navy ship Noa picked john up. He was safe! John glenn became a hero.

MONDAY   **WEEK 12**

- names of places, spacecraft, and ships
- dates

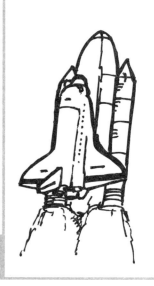

John was born on july 18 1921, in cambridge, Ohio. He wint to college. john then became a Marine Corps pilot. He fought in two wars. he got many medals for his service. on april 9 1959, John became one of the first astronauts. At first, he was a backup pilot. He provided backup for astronauts virgil Grissom and Alan shephard.

TUESDAY   **WEEK 12**

- names of places
- dates

John did other work for the space program He helped design cockpits for the Apollo spacecraft. John retired from the space program on january 16 1964. He retired from the Marine Corps on january 1 1965. In 1974, john became a United States senator for the state of ohio. He served in the Senate for twenny-five years.

- names of places
- dates

WEDNESDAY   **WEEK 12**

On october 29 1998, John became the oldest person to fly in space. He was a crew member on the Discovery a space shuttle. He wanted to sea how space affected older people. Vice President al Gore watched the launch at a school named for glenn. The shuttle landed in florida on november 7 1998. At 77, John was a hero again.

- names of places and spacecraft
- dates

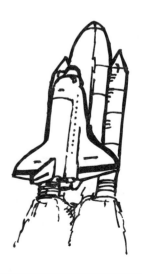

THURSDAY   **WEEK 12**

Write the life story, or biography, of a famous person or of someone you know. Tell about things that happened during the person's life. Give information about the person's family, where the person lived, and any important dates in the person's life. Explain what made this person special. Be sure to use capital letters for people's names, and to use commas to separate numbers in dates and between the names of cities and states.

_____

_____

_____

_____

_____

_____

_____

_____

Chief Seattle and the Settlers

Seattle saw his first white man wen he was a young boy. A ship called the HMS Discovery sailed into Puget Sound. Seattle lived there with his tribe. Seattles father, chief schweabe took him on board the ship. captain George vancouver gave Seattle a treat. seattle decided that some white people were nice.

WATCH FOR

- names of ships and people
- commas

MONDAY   **WEEK 13**

At 21, Seattle became the tribes chief. By that time, many settlers were moving to the Pacific Northwest. They liked the Puget sound area. Seattle invited Isaac N. Ebey and B. F Shaw to live there. He tawt the settler's to fish for salmon and he helped them build houses. In the winter, he gave them food.

WATCH FOR

- people's names and initials
- commas

TUESDAY   **WEEK 13**

chief Seattle started a fishery with Mr. charles Fay. He was from San francisco. Seattle and mr. David S maynard then opened a fishery. It was near the shore of Elliott bay. Many settlers moved there. They liked the helpfull chief so they named their town after him. seattle is now the biggest city in washington state.

WATCH FOR

- people's names, initials, and titles
- commas

WEDNESDAY   **WEEK 13**

Soon, the United States' wanted to bye his tribe's land. Chief Seattle met with Territorial Governor isaac stevens at Point elliott. They signed a treaty and Seattle sold over two million acres of land. The land became the white settlers land. Until his deth, chief Seattle kept his friendship with the settlers.

WATCH FOR

- people's names and titles
- commas

THURSDAY   **WEEK 13**

Describe Chief Seattle's friendship with the white settlers. Explain how he felt about the settlers, and why he felt that way. Tell about the ways he helped the settlers. Tell what the settlers did to honor Chief Seattle. Begin with one of these topic sentences, or write your own:

- Chief Seattle was a friend to the white settlers.

- The white settlers were lucky to know Chief Seattle.

- Chief Seattle helped the settlers in many ways.

_____

_____

_____

_____

_____

_____

_____

_____

Shea and the Leprechaun

- dialog
- commas

"happy St. Patrick's Day, mom! i am going to ketch a leprechaun!" shouted Shea.

"good luck, its tricky!" said her mother. Shea got her dog, Jigs. They ran to the field of wild damp grass.

"once granny said she almost caught a leprechaun here," Shea told Jigs. "Lets find him. i want his gold."

MONDAY   WEEK 14

Suddenly, Shea heard a low quiet laugh coming from behind a tall broad tree. "that may be the leprechaun granny saw," she said to Jigs. "Dont bark while i look."

- dialog
- commas

Shea peeked around the tree she saw a tiny knee-high man in green clothes she ran from behind the tree and grabed him. Shea said, "leprechaun! i want your gold!"

TUESDAY   WEEK 14

"you caught me! Youre much quicker than granny," said the leprechaun. "let go of me and I will tell you where to find a full heavy bag of gold."

Shea lett go. "go to the smooth round rock in the center of the buttercup patch. Thats whare the gold is," he told her. "now its all yours. Youll be very, very rich."

- dialog
- commas

WEDNESDAY   **WEEK 14**

Shea and Jigs serched all around. They didnt find gold. All they saw was a field of silky fluttering flowers. Shea ran backe to the tree, but the leprechaun wasnt there.

"next time, I wont be fooled!" she yelled into the air. "now its time to go home," she said to Jigs. "Well tell mom, dad, and granny. Theyll have ideas for next year."

- dialog
- commas

THURSDAY   **WEEK 14**

FRIDAY   **WEEK 14**

When Shea got home, she told her family about what happened when she and Jigs went looking for the leprechaun. Write one or two paragraphs that tell what Shea said to her family and how they responded. Be sure to use quotation marks for the words spoken by Shea or other people.

_____

_____

_____

_____

_____

_____

_____

_____

_____

_____

_____

Undercover Bugs

• questions

A patch of berrys gleams in the sun. you would loves to taste a ripe berry. You stop to look for the best one. Then a branch on the bush seeming to move. surprise! The branch is not really moving it is an insect! You have just met a walking stick. Can you guess why it have that name

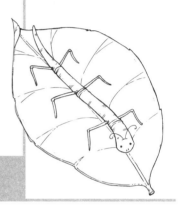

MONDAY   WEEK 15

• questions

walking sticks are insects that look like twigs or tiney branches. They has six legs. some walking sticks can fold up their legs to look even more like a twig. Did you know that they eat only leaves. Some like berry leaves others eats cherry leaves. Some people keep walking sticks as pets some of these pets eat lettuce leaves.

TUESDAY   WEEK 15

The longest insect in the world are a walking stick. it's about 13 inchus long. Walking sticks that are kept as pets are not usually that big Pet walking sticks may grow to be about 6 inches long. When they first comes out of their hard eggshells, they can be as small as half an inch. have you ever saw anything that small

• questions

WEDNESDAY   **WEEK 15**

As insects grow, they sheds their hard outer covering. as the walking stick becomes too small for its growing body, a new, bigger covering taking the place of the old one. a walking stick may shed its covering up to five times before it becomes an adult. Some teechers keep walking sticks as class pets do you think you would like one in your class

• questions

THURSDAY   **WEEK 15**

FRIDAY   **WEEK 15**

Write what you know about walking sticks. Be sure to tell about how they look, how they grow, and what they eat. Begin with one of these topic sentences, or write your own:

- The longest insect on Earth is the walking stick.

- Have you ever seen an insect that looks just like a twig?

- Walking sticks actually have more in common with insects than with plants.

_____

_____

_____

_____

_____

_____

_____

_____

Short Tall Tales

"Babes Disappearing River" by mr. S P royce

    One hot dry June, babe and paul were in oregon. Babe had gone for six and two-thirds days without water. He saw a clean sparkling river. Babe drank for one and one half hour's. He drank nine tenths of the water. That river is now ownly two and three fourths feet deep.

- story titles
- commas
- hyphens

MONDAY   **WEEK 16**

"babe goes dancing by Ms R M brown"

    Babe was in minnesota in july. paul bunyan was playing the fiddle. babe liked Pauls cheerful lively musick. He danced for five and one half days. His dancing heavy feet made 10,000 holes in the ground. Then it rained for four fifths of a month. The holes became lake's.

- story titles
- commas
- hyphens

TUESDAY   **WEEK 16**

"paul and babe in Hollwood by ms. J A mills

Paul and babe went to hollywood in may. They were on amazing people and pets the TV show. There was a strong scary earthquake. Five sixths of california fell into the pacific ocean. Paul and babe put it back. They then starred in a movie called california's heroes.

WATCH FOR

- story titles
- titles of TV shows
- commas
- hyphens

WEDNESDAY   **WEEK 16**

Babe helps johnny inkslinger" by Mr J D post

Johnnys fountain pen broke in march. babe went to the Everglades in florida. He brought back some stalks of dry hollow grass. Each one was about three fifths of a mile long. johnny filled one with nine hundred and two thirds gallons of ink. He wrote and sang "Babes ballad.

WATCH FOR

- story and song titles
- commas
- hyphens

THURSDAY   **WEEK 16**

FRIDAY   **WEEK 16**

Use your imagination! Write another short story for the book <u>The Adventures of Paul and Babe</u>. Tell about something that Paul Bunyan and Babe the Blue Ox did. Explain how they made or changed something in nature. You might tell about how they made mountains, valleys, plains, or deserts. Tell when and where the adventure happened. Give the story a title.

_____

_____

_____

_____

_____

_____

_____

_____

Hand-Me-Downs

On monday, an enormous carton arrived for ginny. It was from peggy and tina her cousins. The karten was full of their used clothes.

ginny said mom do i have to keep these clothes. I don't like Peggys old sweaters. I don't want to wear Tinas jeans.

- commas
- dialog
- questions

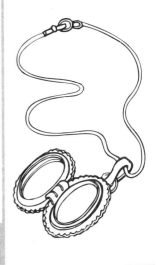

MONDAY   **WEEK 17**

mom said "ginny won't you please wear them! Your cousins clothes are like new, and they're the write size.

ginny said, "okay mom. I would just like to have something new, too.

"mom said, would you like to go shopping on saturday. We can find something to go with the clothes."

- commas
- dialog
- questions

TUESDAY   **WEEK 17**

ginny "said," can we really. Thanks mom.

On saturday, they went shopping. ginny held up a pear of suspenders and a T-shirt. She said "mom I think these would look super with Tinas jeans.

mom said marvelous! How do you like this skirt. It matches one of Peggys' sweaters. Let's buy everything.

- commas
- dialog
- questions

WEDNESDAY   **WEEK 17**

On sunday, mom said "ginny this is another hand-me-down. She showed ginny a silver locket. mom said, this was Nanas and then Grandmothers. grandmother gave it to me. It will be yours someday.

ginny said thanks Mom. Your familys locket is special. Now I understand a hand-me-dow'ns importance.

- commas
- dialog

THURSDAY   **WEEK 17**

Write a story based on something from your own life. Tell what happened. Tell who was with you. You may want to change the real names to other names. Make up quotations to tell what people said. Use one of these ideas, or make up one of your own:

- Tell about something funny that happened.

- Tell about a time you learned a lesson.

- Tell about a gift you received.

How to Skate Safely

how do you buy skates First, wear your skating socks when you try on skates. Second, kick your feet into the backs of the boots After that, buckle the boots and stand up! Next, make sure your toes arent squashed. last, make sure your heel doesnt slide up and down.

From <u>Safe skating magazine</u> by Mike Hulon

MONDAY   **WEEK 18**

What kind of safety equipment should you buy buy wrist guards with plastic plates for wrist protection Get elbow and knee guards in case of falls. The most important thing is a padded helmet! make sure its snug. you dont want a head injury. Now youre reddy to roll

From skate equipment today by Tracy Hill

TUESDAY   **WEEK 18**

how can you skate for fitness. For your safety, go to a flat, paved area! Don't' go near traffic. Dont go down hills if you cant' stop. do five minutes of slow skateing as a warm-up Next, skate rapidly for twenty minutes. skate slowly for five minnets to cool down. Youll' feel super?

From fitness skating magazine By Kim scott

WEATCH FOR
- questions
- apostrophes
- magazine titles

WEDNESDAY   WEEK 18

How do you fall harmlessly first, bend forward at the waist. Second, bend your knees. Third, touch your knee guards Next, slide forward onto your protective gear. keep your hedd up to avoid facial scrapes. at the same time, let your body slide flat on the ground. Youre safe

From athletic safeguards by Matt todd

WEATCH FOR
- questions
- apostrophes
- magazine titles

THURSDAY   WEEK 18

Write directions for the safe use of your in-line skates. The directions can include how to buy skates and gear, how to skate for fitness, and how to fall safely. Explain the steps in order. Use sequence words in your directions. Begin with one of these topic sentences, or write your own:

- How can you use your in-line skates safely?

- Here are some suggestions for safe skating.

- Skating can be fun and safe, too.

_____

_____

_____

_____

_____

_____

_____

Meg's Prize

- dialog
- colons in time
- titles of TV shows

At 400 p:m one day in 1955, Meg Burns walked into the house and yelled "mom you wont believe this I won a television set! We have the furst TV on the block!

Doris Burns said my how lucky good for you Meg.

Meg said now we can watch the mighty mouse playhouse and I Love Lucy right here at home.

MONDAY   **WEEK 19**

Meg called out dad come look at this Rich come here!

- dialog
- colons in time
- titles of TV shows

It was 4,30 P.M. and american bandstand was just starting. They heard voices singing "bandstand boogie. Dick Clark appeared on the tiny screen and said hello heres our show for today. Meet our teenage dancers.

Meg said Im going to dance along with them.

TUESDAY   **WEEK 19**

At 530, Rich wanted to watch The howdy doody show. They all sang along to Its howdy doody time.

Rich said wow Howdy Doody is a funny puppet. They watched city newsreel from 6,00 until 700 pM: "the milton berle show" was on next. They laughed at the funny actors until 800 P.m

WATCH FOR
- dialog
- colons in time
- titles of TV shows

WEDNESDAY   **WEEK 19**

The family watched Roy Rogers and Dale Evans ride their horses during The roy rogers Show. At the end of the show, they sang happy trails to you.

At 900 pm, Meg said mom we havent had dinner yet."

we'll have to learn to use this TV wisely said Mrs. Burns. otherwise, well never get anything done

WATCH FOR
- dialog
- colons in time
- titles of TV shows

THURSDAY   **WEEK 19**

"Meg's Prize" is a historical fiction story. It combines the real names of early TV shows and their theme songs with a story about a family's first TV set. Write your own historical fiction story. Tell about something that really happened. Add characters that you make up.

_____

_____

_____

_____

_____

_____

_____

_____

_____

_____

The Blizzard of 2003

Washington, D.C.   February 16, 2003

• names of places
• abbreviations

Residents of the nations capital woke up to a winter wonderland this morening. A huge storm system came through West virginia into the washington DC area on saturday. By sunday afternoon, about 60 centimeters (2 ft) of snow cuvvered the ground. Cars were stuck on new york Avenue and other streets.

MONDAY	**WEEK 20**

bob T Stone was in mt vernon square. He was makeing a snowman and singing frosty the snowman. He said, its great my snowman is 182 centimeters (6 ft) high

• dialog
• names of places
• abbreviations

ms meg f moore and her dog were walking on K St to a friends house. Her dog was catching snowflakes and she was singging let it snow.

TUESDAY	**WEEK 20**

jeff a hanks said my cars' roof has 71 centimeters (28 in) of snow on it. Iv'e never scene anything like this Im from monterey california. mr hanks was to fly home today but baltimore-washington international airport is closed. He may not get out until tuesday.

WATCH FOR
- dialog
- names of places
- abbreviations

WEDNESDAY   **WEEK 20**

dr ann T green said Four-wheel-drive cars are needed. If drivers can help we're looking for people to give hospital workers rides. We needs the public's help.

Weather forecaster dave R coons said The storm is moving north and dover delaware, may get 60 centimeters (2 ft,) of snow by monday. Stay inside and keep saif."

WATCH FOR
- dialog
- names of places
- abbreviations

THURSDAY   **WEEK 20**

Write a news story about a storm in your area. Tell when and where the storm took place. If there was rain or snow, tell how much fell. Explain what happened because of the storm. Use quotes from people that tell what they saw, did, or felt. Remember to keep to the facts. Don't add your own opinion.

_____

_____

_____

_____

_____

_____

_____

_____

_____

How to Make a Sand Sundae

WATCH FOR
- abbreviations
- commas

Whats a sand sundae? Its a cool way to display a photo. Heres how to make one. First, get the supplies. Youll need several clear plastic glasses or you can use glass jars. They should be 10–15 centimeters (4-6 in) tall. Also, get about 155 grams (5 oz) of colored sand and 124 grams (4 oz) of white candil wax for each sundae.

MONDAY   **WEEK 21**

Second, get some 4 by 6 centimeter ($1\frac{1}{2}$ in by $2\frac{1}{2}$ in) photos. Place a foto against the inside of the glass but make sure it faces the outside of the glass. Use a little bit of clear tape on the sides of the photo and itll stay in place. Use more than one photo if theyll fit.

WATCH FOR
- abbreviations
- commas

TUESDAY   **WEEK 21**

Third, add the sand use different colors to make a design. Use about 31 grams (1 oz) each of 4 or 5 colors. To start, put won color into the glass. Next, add a layer of another color. After that, put in the next color Finaly, add the last color. Tilt the glass to make curves or use a toothpick. To push one color into another.

- abbreviations
- commas

WEDNESDAY   **WEEK 21**

Forth, make the topping but get help from an adult. To start, melt the candle wax in a pot. Next, beet it with a eggbeater until its foamy. After that, spoon the wax onto the top of the sand. Let it drip over a bit and itll look like real whipped cream. Finally, give your "sand sundae" to someone you like or keep it for yourself!

- commas

THURSDAY   **WEEK 21**

Write directions that tell how to make a sandwich, scrambled eggs, or something else you like to eat. Be sure to list the ingredients. Tell the amount of each ingredient needed, too. Give the steps for making the food in order. Use number sequence words like **first**, **second**, and **third**, or use other sequence words like **next**, **then**, and **after that**.

Poetry Book Reviews

where the sidewalk ends by S. Silverstein has 127 poems about food people animals and other things. mr Silverstein's rhymes are clever and his drawings are funny. "the Crocodiles toothache" has a surprise ending. The unicorn was made into a song. Heres a book to share with your family friends and teachers

- titles of books and poems
- commas

MONDAY　　　　　　　　　　　　**WEEK 22**

---

grandmother's nursery rhymes by N P Jaramillo has rhymes riddles and lullabies. You can reed them in English or you can read them in Spanish "Grandfathers Poem" is gentle. the spider" is a riddle about nature. You'll enjoy reading ms Jaramillos rhymes and youll be delighted by ms Savadier's colorful drawings.

- titles of books and poems
- commas

TUESDAY　　　　　　　　　　　　**WEEK 22**

The funny poems in A Poem for a Pickle by E Merriam will make you giggle laugh and chuckle. The poems have a great beat and youll want to dance while you read them. The poem "urban rainbow describes colors in the city. The book Can a can has words with more than one meaning Youd' better read this great book

- titles of books and poems
- commas

WEDNESDAY   **WEEK 22**

The book The dragons are singing tonight by J prelutsky has 17 poems for dragon fans. mr Prelutsky's poems rhyme and they are fun to say aloud. Theres an upset dragon in the poem "A Dragons lament. The dragon in Im an amiable dragon" is friendly. You should get this book and then you should read it to your favrit dragon

- titles of books and poems
- commas

THURSDAY   **WEEK 22**

Write a review of a poetry book or another book you have read recently. Give the title of the book and the author's name. Be sure to underline the book's title. For a poetry book, describe a few of the poems and give their titles. Don't forget to use quotation marks around the titles of poems. For other books, describe their main focus. Tell what you like or don't like about the book. Tell readers why they should or should not read this book.

_____

_____

_____

_____

_____

_____

_____

_____

_____

The Boston Tea Party

in 1773, the king of england put a tax on the paper paint lead glass and tea sent to the colonies in america.

"we cant vote for or against the tax, so we should'nt have to pay it the colonists in boston said to each other. they refused to buy the taxed goods after a while, the British took away all but the tax on tea.

• dialog
• commas

MONDAY   **WEEK 23**

the colonists wouldnt buy the tea or pay the tax One evening, angry people gathered in the meeting house. A man yelled "the hated tea is now on ships in our harbor

someone shouted lets show King George how we feel."

"boston harbor will be a teapot tonight cried the crowd.

• dialog
• exclamations

TUESDAY   **WEEK 23**

A groope of men dressed up like Indians. They wore face paint blankets and feathers. They got on the ships they picked up the tea chests. They used hammers knives and shovels to smash the chests. they then dumped the tea into the water. as they left, they chanted tell king george wel'l pay no taxes on his tea."

- dialog
- commas
- exclamations

WEDNESDAY   **WEEK 23**

King George was angerie about the tea. he closed the harbor outlawed meetings and put soldiers in the city. He thought the colonists would give in.

this means war" shouted the colonists. We will rule ourselves from now on. the colonists won the war. There wouldnt be a king they would vote for laws and taxes.

- dialog
- commas
- exclamations

THURSDAY   **WEEK 23**

FRIDAY   **WEEK 23**

Tell what you know about the Boston Tea Party. Explain why the colonists were angry. Tell what they did about their problems. Tell how King George felt about the colonists' actions and how he treated them. Begin with one of these topic sentences, or write your own:

- A tax on tea caused a war.

- The Boston Tea Party showed how the colonists felt about King George's taxes.

_____

_____

_____

_____

_____

_____

_____

_____

_____

Letters Home

- names of places and ships
- hyphens

Dear tilly

    I got to new york city new york, one-half month ago. It was a tiring lonely ride over on the ship, the SS Ford. I was seasick for about one third of the voyage. For the first week, I stayed at 64 E ninth St I miss you but I like this friendly exciting country. You will join me soon

Dear Tilly,
  I will be leaving for America in the morning. I won't know the ship's name until I get to the dock tomorrow.
  My only concern is seasickness.
  I miss you so much!
  Your loving husband,
  Anders

MONDAY   **WEEK 24**

    I met a man named nick in new york. Thanks to him, I got a job at a steel mill in pittsburgh pennsylvania. It took one half of my money for the train ticket but I got there I stayed at 112 N oak Ave with nick

    Your loving Husband

    anders

- names of places
- hyphens

TUESDAY   **WEEK 24**

Dear tilly

I have a new job on a large ship It is named the USS Traveler. I shovel cole and I keep the ship's powerful hungry engines running It was a busy hard trip from new york to san francisco california. I worrk for two thirds of each day After work, I ride cable cars on hyde St and powell St

- names of places and ships
- hyphens

WEDNESDAY **WEEK 24**

I will send for you in three fourths of a year. You can take the ship, the SS Hanson to new york city. The "USS Traveler" will be there and we will take it to portland oregon. I bought a farm there on maple Rd for us

Your Loving husband

anders

- names of places and ships
- hyphens

Dear Tilly,
I will be leaving for America in the morning. I won't know the ship's name until I get to the dock tomorrow.
My only concern is seasickness.
I miss you so much!
Your loving husband,
Anders

THURSDAY **WEEK 24**

FRIDAY   **WEEK 24**

Choose one of these ideas and write another letter:

- Write a letter from Anders to Tilly. Tell about the work Anders did on the trip from San Francisco to California.

- Write a letter from Tilly to Anders. Tell about Tilly's preparations for the trip to America.

- Write a letter from Anders to Tilly. Tell what Anders wants to do when the family reaches Portland, Oregon.

_____

_____

_____

_____

_____

_____

_____

_____

The Boy Who Cried Wolf

Long ugo, there was a young shepherd boy. He tooked care of the sheep. He made shure they was safe and didnt wander off alone. The job was boring, so the boy played a trick on the village people. He stood on a tree stump and yelled "Wolf! Wolf A wolf is after the sheep!

- dialog
- exclamations

MONDAY   **WEEK 25**

The villagers grabed rakes and sticks. They ran to the hillside The boy laughed at them and said, Silly villagers There are no wolf. Its a joke I made up."

The villagers didnt think it was funny. Dont play tricks on us" one man said. The villagers then went back to their work.

- dialog
- exclamations

TUESDAY   **WEEK 25**

A few days later, the boy were bored again. He wondered if his trick would work wonce more. The boy standed on the stump and cried "Wolf Wolf! I need help!

Again the villagirs ran to help the boy. "Ha, ha! I fooled you" laughed the shepherd boy.

"Were angry about your mean tricks, they told him.

WATCH FOR

- dialog
- exclamations

WEDNESDAY   **WEEK 25**

The next day begane peacefully. Then a wolf really did attack the sheep. The boy jumped onto the stump and yelled, "A wolf are killing the sheep? I mean it

"I wont be fooled again, said one villager.

Neither will we" said the others. They all went back two work. The poor shepherd boy watched the wolf eats his sheep

WATCH FOR

- dialog
- exclamations

THURSDAY   **WEEK 25**

Think about "The Boy Who Cried Wolf," and then write one or two paragraphs about this fable. What lesson do you think the boy learned by the end of the story? How do you think he will act in the future? Do you think the villagers will ever trust him again? Be sure to give several reasons to support or explain your response.

_____

_____

_____

_____

_____

_____

_____

_____

Welcome to the Arctic Tundra

The arctic tundra is the coldest and dryest biome I'ts around the north pole. There are also tundra areas in europe asia and North america. Theres about one-half foot of rain there each year The growing season is one sixth of a year long. The temperature is beloe 32 degrees for about ten twelfths of the year

MONDAY   **WEEK 26**

About 1,700 kinds of plants grow in the tundra One fourth of the plants have flowers The other three fourths of the plants are shrubs mosses sedges and grasses. Their roots cant go very deep A layer of permafrost is one half foot below the surface. The frozen ground wont let water get into the soil below it

TUESDAY   **WEEK 26**

• names of places
• commas

Plant-eeting animals such as caribou hares and squirrels live in the tundra The foxes wolves and polar bears eat meat. Arctic animals have short bodies extra fat and thick fur. They dont get too cold. Most of the animals sleep all winter The caribou live in canada greenland and alaska

WEDNESDAY   **WEEK 26**

• names of places
• commas

Ravens falcons loons and snowbirds live in the tundra These birds dont always stay there They fly south for the winter. Some fly to canada. The snowy owls fly all the way to virginia. There arent many snakes lizards or frogs. The wether isnt warm enough for them Cod trout salmon and other fish live in the cold waters

THURSDAY   **WEEK 26**

FRIDAY | **WEEK 26**

Write one or two paragraphs that describe the Arctic tundra. Be sure to say where it is located, what the climate is like, and the types of plants and animals that live there. Start with one of these topic sentences, or write one of your own:

- The Arctic tundra is a cold, dry place.

- The animals of the Arctic tundra are adapted to the cold.

- Do you think plants and animals can live in a cold, frozen land?

_____

_____

_____

_____

_____

_____

_____

_____

Liak, an Inuit Girl

- names of people and places
- commas

my name is Liak. I am Inuit (IN–oo–it). The inuit are people who live in the cold arctic lands in alaska canada and greenland. I live with mom dad and my brothers. Moms name is noayak. Dads names is baral. My brothers names are qayak and tuma. our family. And friends have always lived here

MONDAY   **WEEK 27**

- commas

winter here is long dark and very cold. It lasts from october until march. My family and I wear his warm parkas watertight boots and thick glove. I like the summer, especially july and august. we have sunshine all day and night my friends and I play outside a lot. Moms flower garden is beautiful

TUESDAY   **WEEK 27**

my ancestors homes was huts or tents they traveled By foots, dogsled or boat. They hunted whales seals and walruses. I have an easier life my families house is modern We use snowmobiles cars airplanes and motorboats. mom and dad buy our food at a big store. I buy clothes CDs and video games there, too

• commas

WEDNESDAY   **WEEK 27**

mom and dad are teacher. my two brother and I go to school We learn math reading science English and our native language. qayak makes inuit carvings. he sells them in many stores at craft fairs and on the Internet. Tumas' hobbies is playing the guitar I like to teach the old Inuit storys, legends and songs to others

• commas

THURSDAY   **WEEK 27**

Daily Paragraph Editing • EMC 6803 • © Evan-Moor Corp.

Write a personal narrative like Liak's. Tell about your family. Describe the place where you live. Tell about some of the things you like to do. Begin with one of these topic sentences, or write your own:

- My name is _____.

- My life is very interesting.

- Let me introduce myself.

_____

_____

_____

_____

_____

_____

_____

_____

_____

_____

_____

_____

The Dog Ate My Homework

It was a bright sunny saturday. The phone rang, and I anserd. My friend, tina, was on the line.

Tina said "can you go to the recreation center, kendra. sally, keesha, and me are going.

I moaned and said I cant. Im on restriction. Heres my story.

- commas
- questions
- dialog

MONDAY   **WEEK 28**

On tuesday, mr. hobson said Wheres' your homework, kendra johnson. Please give him to me.

I replied, my silly hungry dog ate it.

On wednesday, Mr hobson said where is you homework, Kendra! Did you ferget it?

"I said," my mean cranky brother matt tore it.

- commas
- questions
- dialog

TUESDAY   **WEEK 28**

On thursday, Mr hobson asked, do you have your homework, did you bring it today?"

I told him, no, it went down the kitchen sink. Ms reston, the young new plumber, couldnt get it out.

mr. Hobson asked me again on friday. I answered I was too feverish to work. I needed to relax.

- commas
- questions
- dialog

WEDNESDAY   **WEEK 28**

mr. hobson called my mom. He said "Mrs johnson, kendra hasnt turned in her homework all week.

He put me on the telephone. "Mom said why didnt you do your work thats a careless, irresponsible way to behave. youll finish it on saturday and sunday.

I learned my lesson I wont skip homework ever again!

- commas
- questions
- dialog

THURSDAY   **WEEK 28**

Choose one of these ideas and write a personal narrative:

- Pretend you are Kendra. Write about the time that you did not do your homework.

- Pretend you are Kendra. Write about another adventure you had.

- Write about yourself. Tell about something that happened to you.

_____

_____

_____

_____

_____

_____

_____

_____

A Holiday Diary

december, 25 2003

dear diary

Its christmas day I have a new diary Im so excited! I cant wait to right every day. Ill tell about things that happen. I will also draw some pictures Theyl'l go with the words I want to be an author and illustrator when i grow up. this diary will be a good place to practice

WATCH FOR
- dates
- salutations
- holidays

MONDAY   **WEEK 29**

---

december 26. 2003

dear diary

Hooray today is the first day of kwanzaa Our family celebrates it after christmas. it lasts for seven days. dad said that this holiday started in America in 1966 Each day, we talk about ways to make our lives better we also light a candle

WATCH FOR
- dates
- salutations
- holidays
- exclamations

TUESDAY   **WEEK 29**

december 31 2003

dear diary.

Its the sixth day of kwanzaa we spent the past for days at grandma and grandpa's house We all had a fun time. each evening, we celebrated together. We lit the candles ate lots of good food and listened to music from Africa. I didnt have time to write in my diary

- dates
- salutations
- holidays

WEDNESDAY   **WEEK 29**

january 1 2004

dear diary

Wow today is the last day of kwanzaa Its a day to celebrate faith. mom says that faith is believing that good things will happen Also, today is new year's day. I have one new year's resolution. I will write in my diary every week, thats a promise

- dates
- salutations
- holidays
- exclamations

THURSDAY   **WEEK 29**

Choose one of these ideas and write a diary entry:

- Write an entry for January 2nd. Tell about the family celebration for the last night of Kwanzaa on January 1st.

- Write an entry for January 8th. Tell about the first day back at school after vacation.

- Write a diary entry about your own life. Tell about something that you did or how you felt about something.

_____

_____

_____

_____

_____

_____

_____

_____

Who Ya Gonna Call? Robot Helpers!

Who does work that people don't do? Robots, that's who Robots are machines that have computers inside them they can move. They have sensors that let them see hear and touch things. People program robbots. the robots then do their jobs. Robots drill holes spray paint and put together cars. Wow! thats a lot of work.

MONDAY   **WEEK 30**

Do robots help with disasters? Yes, they sure do There was an accident in a nuclear power plant the building wasnt safe for people. A robot went in cleaned up the mess and came out safely.

Have you ever seen a fallen building Robots can look through the rubble find victims and signal rescuers

TUESDAY   **WEEK 30**

Daily Paragraph Editing • EMC 6803 • © Evan-Moor Corp.

How do robots help the space program? Astronauts couldn't go to Mars, but a robot did It collected rocks read temperatures and took pictures. A robot camera is now looking for life on other planets It takes pictures records information and sends it all back to the scientists. Goodness thats a big job

WATCH FOR
- commas
- exclamations

WEDNESDAY   **WEEK 30**

What other hard tasks can robots do? robots go where people cant go. They crawl into volcanoes take samples of gases and examine the smoke Robots dive deep in the oceans look at strange creatures and record temperatures. Gee thats dangerous Arent you glad we have robots

WATCH FOR
- commas
- exclamations
- questions

THURSDAY   **WEEK 30**

Write what you know about robots. Be sure to tell what they do to help people. List two or more jobs they can do in one sentence. Begin with one of these topic sentences, or write your own:

- Robots are very helpful.

- If you need a job done, call a robot!

- Did you know that robots have been up in space and down deep in the ocean?

_____

_____

_____

_____

_____

_____

_____

_____

_____

The History of Calendars

Long, long ago, people made the first calendars. To keep track of the seasons These calinders divided the year by the moons cycles. There were a full moon about 12 times between one spring and the next and there were 29 or 30 days between each full moon. The year was divided into 12 lunar months it had 354 days

• commas

MONDAY   **WEEK 31**

The people of babylon used the lunar calendar but They didnt no that there were really 365 days in a year. Their lunar calendar was 11 days short each year After a few years, the seasons and munths didnt match up. Every eight years, three months had to be added The Babylonians got very mixed up!

• commas

TUESDAY   **WEEK 31**

The egyptians looked at the stars in the sky They saw that the Dog Star rose next to the sun every 365 days. They made a calendar and they based it on the sun. This calendar Divided the 365 days into 12 month. This worked well Weve based our calender on the one from ancient egypt.

• commas

WEDNESDAY   **WEEK 31**

An emperor in rome made another calendar with 12 months of 30 or 31 days each He aded a leap year with 80 extra days every four years but this was too confusing.

• commas

In 1582, a math experts changed the Rules for leap year and made the calendar more exact. The season didnt move around anymore. We use this calendar today

THURSDAY   **WEEK 31**

Write what you know about the history of calendars. Be sure to tell when they started. Name the groups of people who made early calendars. Tell a little bit about how calendars have changed, and which is used today. Use one of these topic sentences, or write your own:

- Since early times, people have tried to keep track of time.

- People have used the sun and the moon to make calendars.

_____

_____

_____

_____

_____

_____

_____

_____

Shadows

do you know what makes a shadow First, some light is necessary Next, there has to be something blokking the light. When you are outsied during the day, bright light comes from the sun. if you block the sunlight a shadow will appear on the opposite side of you

- questions
- commas

MONDAY   **WEEK 32**

have you seen your shadow at several different times of the day? What did the size and shape look like The size and shap depend on the sun's location in the sky. if the sun is directly overhead a shadow will be short and fat. if the sun is lower in the sky a shadow will be long and skinny

- questions
- commas

TUESDAY   **WEEK 32**

have you ever been frightened by unusual shadows in your bedroom at night? what do you discover if you turn on more lights Anything that blocks light can create a scary shadow on your wall Shadows are visible even after dark. there has to be a small amount of light shining threw a window to make a shadow

• questions

WEDNESDAY   **WEEK 32**

you can have a great time with shadows. Shine a flashlight on a small object look past the object and you will see its shadow have you ever played shadow tag Wate for a sunny day and then go outside with friends. The person who is "It" tries to step on the other players shadows Playing shadow tag is fun

• questions
• commas

THURSDAY   **WEEK 32**

Write a paragraph that summarizes information about shadows. Explain how they are made and how they change. Start your paragraph with one of these questions, or write your own:

- Have you ever seen shadows in the evening?

- Do you know what causes your shadow to look longer or shorter?

- What makes a shadow?

_____

_____

_____

_____

_____

_____

_____

_____

The Ups and Downs of Roller Coasters

WATCH FOR

- commas

when it comes to speedy roller coasters, gravity rooles! From the very beginning roller coasters have worked by a simply scientific rule: What goes up must come down Gravity makes that happin. Gravity is a natural force. It makes objects move toward Earths center

MONDAY   **WEEK 33**

the first hill of a roller coaster ride has to be the steepest gravity quickly pulls the coaster down that hill. It creates enough energy. For the ride to coste easily along until it comes to another hill. no hill can be higher than the first. It would take more energy to go up the rest of the hills than the cars had at the start

TUESDAY   **WEEK 33**

as coasters fly rapid down hills and arownd curves they create G-forces. A G-force is the heavy pressure riders feel. The original roller coasters were circular they created very strong G-forces. The forces were too hard on people, some got sick. later, tracks in teardrop shapes were tried. They did not cause such powerful G-forces

WEDNESDAY   WEEK 33

• commas
• abbreviations

Today, roller coasters speed down steep hills up to 94.48 meters (310 ft) tall. they hit speeds of up to 100 miles per hour and they may loop up to eight times. rides may be short or long. One-half minute (30 sec) is about the shortest. the longest, so far, is 90 seconds (1½ min) Gravity makes all of these great rides possible

THURSDAY   WEEK 33

Tell what gravity is, and explain how it makes a roller coaster work. Describe the first hill on a roller coaster, and tell why it has to be the highest. Tell about the rest of the ride. Use one of these topic sentences, or write your own:

- Roller coasters need gravity.

- Without gravity, a roller coaster will not go.

- Gravity helps make roller coasters work.

_____

_____

_____

_____

_____

_____

_____

_____

_____

The First Computer Bug

WATCH FOR
- dialog
- commas

On september 9 1945, I was at harvard university to test a knew computer program for the Mark II Calculator.

I said, "Something isnt right here, Dan.

Dan, my co-worker, said "What's that Max?

I said, "The program was supposed to ad, but it subtracted. It was supposed to multiply but it divided.

MONDAY   **WEEK 34**

WATCH FOR
- dialog
- commas

We herd crackling sounds and we saw sparks. The computer wasn't working at all. I took off the machines' glass cover. I said there's a two-inch-long moth Dan. It's stuck between points at Relay 70, Panel F.

Dan said max you found a bug in the computer?

I said Yes Dan. I think it caused our problems

TUESDAY   **WEEK 34**

- dialog
- commas

I removed the moth and then I put the computers cover back on. Dan started the Mark II and it worked!

I taped the bug to the days log page. I rote First actual case of bug being found. september 9 1945."

We told Hopper, our boss, the hole story.

Dan said we debugged the computer Hopper.

WEDNESDAY   **WEEK 34**

- dialog
- commas

Hopper said, guys we just made history! soon, every computer problem was called a "bug"

On september 9 1999, I was at the smithsonian Institution with Dan. We saw a logbook. The books ink hadn't faded and the moth was still taped there.

Dan said max there's our computer bug!

THURSDAY   **WEEK 34**

A historical fiction story uses a real event to tell a story. A worker really did find a moth in a computer, and he called it a "computer bug." The log is displayed in the Smithsonian. Lt. Hopper really was on duty when the moth was found. Dan and Max are made-up characters. Write your own historical fiction story. Use a real event and made-up characters.

_____

_____

_____

_____

_____

_____

_____

_____

_____

Cactus—A Desert Plant

- commas
- abbreviations

Cactuses grow in hot dry deserts. The smallest cactus is about 5 centimeters (2 in) tall. The largest cactus is about 18 meters (60 ft) tall. All cactuses can store water. the water is gathered by roots and then the plant stores it. The roots usually grow down 2.5 centimeters (1 in) to 15 centimeters (6 in) deep in the soil. they absorb water quickly.

MONDAY   **WEEK 35**

- commas
- abbreviations

A cholla cactus has sharp prickly spines. The spines come off easy. Chollas vary in size from 10 centimeters (4 in) to 3 meters (10 ft) tall. Some of their flours are 4 centimeters ($1\frac{1}{2}$ in) wide. pack rats collect the stems and then pile them up in front of their burrows. the stems protect the pack rats from their dangerous hungry enemies.

TUESDAY   **WEEK 35**

The saguaro is the tallest cactus. By the time it is 100 years old, it may be 5 meters (16 ft) tall. It has a smooth waxy fluted stem. it can store up to 200 gallons of water. The water heats slow during the day and the cactus stays cool. The water lets off the heet at night and the cactus stays warm

- commas
- abbreviations

WEDNESDAY   **WEEK 35**

A barrel cactus is shorter and fat than some of the other cactuses. A full-grown one can be 1.5 meters (5 ft) tall and 60 centimeters (24 in) wide. It's stretchy pleated sides let it store water. The barrel cactus gets larger. When it is full of water and smaller as the water is used up. the pulp can be used to make candy

- commas
- abbreviations

THURSDAY   **WEEK 35**

FRIDAY   **WEEK 35**

Write what you know about cactuses. Be sure to tell about their size and about how the different types look. Describe the way the saguaro and barrel cactuses store water. Begin with one of these topic sentences, or write one of your own:

- The cactus is an unusual plant.

- Did you know that plants can grow in the desert?

- A cactus knows how to take the heat.

_____

_____

_____

_____

_____

_____

_____

The Contest

groundhog day was a big day in the town where twins fran and fred lived. Everywon liked to watch phil the groundhog come out of his burrow. The TV station ran a contest. People had to guess the time phil would appear The winners would be on the TV show Hello from Our Town and they would also get a copy of the book <u>groundhogs forever</u>

- titles of books and TV shows
- holidays

MONDAY   **WEEK 36**

Fran and fred read all about groundhog day. they learned that groundhogs come out of their holes on february 2nd. They help predict if there will be six more weeks of winter or if spring will arrive soon. If the groundhog sees his shadow, there will be more winter If there is no shadow, winter will be ending soon

- holidays

TUESDAY   **WEEK 36**

Fran and fred looked at old copies of North Country Magazine and found the times phil had appeared in past years. They decided Phil would come out at 235 pm. Fran entered their guess at 1014 am on january 30th. The station clerk told her to watch the groundhog day special on february 2nd to find out who had winned

WATCH FOR

- titles of magazines and TV shows
- colons in time

WEDNESDAY   **WEEK 36**

The twins got up at 630 am on february 2nd. They thought about phil all day They watched the Groundhog Day Special at 500 pm. What a Surprise! At exactly 235 pm phil came out and saw his shadow. fran and fred had won! They would be on <u>hello from our town</u> and they would also get a copy of Groundhogs Forever.

WATCH FOR

- titles of books and TV shows
- colons in time

THURSDAY   **WEEK 36**

Think about "The Contest," and then write one or two paragraphs about this story. What was the contest about? What were the prizes? What did Fred and Fran do to try to win? How did they find out they had won? Be sure to give examples from the story to support or explain your response.

_____

_____

_____

_____

_____

_____

_____

_____

_____

_____

Proofreading Marks

Use these marks to show corrections.

Mark	Meaning	Example
℘	Take this out (delete).	I love ~~to~~ to read.
⊙	Add a period.	It was late⊙
≡	Make this a capital letter.	First prize went to m<u>a</u>ria.
/	Make this a lowercase letter.	We saw a B̸lack C̸at.
———	Fix the spelling.	This is our ~~hause~~ house.
∧	Add a comma.	Goodnight∧ Mom.
⌄	Add an apostrophe.	It⌄s mine.
⌄⌄ ⌄⌄	Add quotation marks.	⌄⌄Come in,⌄⌄ he said.
!∧ ?∧	Add an exclamation point or a question mark.	Help!∧Can you help me?∧
⊼	Add a hyphen.	I've read three⊼fourths of the book.
⌒	Close the space.	Foot⌒ball is fun.
∧	Add a word.	The ∧pen is mine. (red)
———	Underline the words.	We read <u>Old Yeller</u>.
∴∧	Add a colon.	Alex arrived at 4∧00.

Daily Paragraph Editing • EMC 6803 • © Evan-Moor Corp.

Editing Checklist

Use this checklist to review and revise your writing:

◯	Does each sentence begin with a capital letter?
◯	Do names of people and places begin with a capital letter?
◯	Does each sentence end with a period, a question mark, or an exclamation point?
◯	Did I use apostrophes to show possession (*Ana's desk*) and in contractions (*isn't*)?
◯	Did I choose the correct word (*to, too, two*)?
◯	Did I check for spelling errors?
◯	Did I place commas where they are needed?
◯	Are my sentences clear and complete?